YOUR KNOWLEDGE HAS VALUE

Ayoub Kafyulilo, Fidelice M.S. Mafumiko

Implications of Childhood overweight and obesity on learning behaviour and classroom performance

GRIN Verlag

Bibliografische Information der Deutschen Nationalbibliothek:

Die Deutsche Bibliothek verzeichnet diese Publikation in der Deutschen National-
bibliografie; detaillierte bibliografische Daten sind im Internet über http://dnb.d-
nb.de/ abrufbar.

Dieses Werk sowie alle darin enthaltenen einzelnen Beiträge und Abbildungen
sind urheberrechtlich geschützt. Jede Verwertung, die nicht ausdrücklich vom
Urheberrechtsschutz zugelassen ist, bedarf der vorherigen Zustimmung des Verla-
ges. Das gilt insbesondere für Vervielfältigungen, Bearbeitungen, Übersetzungen,
Mikroverfilmungen, Auswertungen durch Datenbanken und für die Einspeicherung
und Verarbeitung in elektronische Systeme. Alle Rechte, auch die des auszugsweisen
Nachdrucks, der fotomechanischen Wiedergabe (einschließlich Mikrokopie) sowie
der Auswertung durch Datenbanken oder ähnliche Einrichtungen, vorbehalten.

Imprint:

Copyright © 2010 GRIN Verlag GmbH
Druck und Bindung: Books on Demand GmbH, Norderstedt Germany
ISBN: 978-3-656-20583-8

This book at GRIN:

http://www.grin.com/en/e-book/194198/implications-of-childhood-overweight-and-
obesity-on-learning-behaviour

Implications of Childhood overweight and obesity on learning behaviour and classroom performance

Ayoub C. Kafyulilo and Fidelice M.S. Mafumiko

Department of Curriculum and Teaching, Faculty of Education

Dar es Salaam University College of Education-*A constituent college of the University of Dar es Salaam*)

Abstract

This article is based on a study carried out from October, 2007 to May, 2008 that investigated the extent to which overweight and obesity were challenges among primary school children in Kinondoni and Njombe Districts in Tanzania. Systematic random sampling was used to select schools while stratified sampling and simple random sampling were used in selecting pupils and teachers who participated in the study. Measurement of weights and heights was done to determine Body Mass Index (BMI), while measurement of skin folds was done to determine body fat percentage. Close-ended questionnaires, semi-structured interviews and focus group discussions were used to collect data on the implications of overweight and obesity on health and learning behaviours. Findings of the study revealed that an average of 13.5% of children were overweight or obese. Hypertension, excessive sweating, teasing and peer rejection were common to obese children. In addition, overweight and obese children were reported to perform less than their peers in academic and physical activities. This study rerecommends among other things the establishment of education programs through mass media to raise people's awareness of how overweight and obesity affects children's health, social and classroom learning behaviours as well as performance.

Background

Overweight and obesity are worldwide problems now days. Tanzania, like many countries in the world, is currently experiencing the problem of overweight and obesity not only among adults, but also in children. Literature shows that a high percentage of the world's population is overweight or obese, with the USA having 50%, Australia 37%, Western Europe 30% and India 17% (Gavin, 2005). According to WHO (2005), this may mean that, a big number of worlds' population is at risk of developing cancer, cardiovascular diseases, non-insulin-dependent diabetes, severe articular dysfunctions, and hypertensions worldwide.

Overweight and obese children are reported to be at risk of serious health conditions such as high cholesterol, insulin resistance, bone problems, joint problems and shortness of breath, which make exercise and physical activity difficult (Johnson, 2002). Accordingly, problems of restless or disordered sleep patterns and tendency to mature earlier than usual are common to overweight and obese children. Overweight girls may experience irregular menstrual cycles that can lead to fertility problems in adulthood. Gall bladder diseases and depression are also common to overweight and obese children (Ekblom, 2005). Overweight and obese children may also become more susceptible to easy fracture due to osteoporosis and too much weight that cannot be sustained by leg bones (Gavin, 2005; Diertz, 1998). Accordingly, many people have been suffering from degenerative diseases of weight-bearing joints, such as knees. Such problems were once considered exclusively adult diseases. Pains in the lower back are also common in obese people and may be one of the major contributors to obesity-related absenteeism from work and schools (Newbold, 2004).

There are other several risks associated with childhood overweight and obesity. Johnson (2002) describe that overweight and obesity entail health risks to the affected individual and the public. The Australian Institute of Health and Welfare (2004) lists the relationship between different body weight level and associated 'co-morbidities' or health risks (see Table 1).

Table 1: Classification of Body Mass Index (BMI) versus Risk Level

BMI (kg/m2)	Classification	Risk of comorbidities
Less than 18.5	Underweight	Low (but increase risk of other clinical problems)
18.5 to less than 25	Normal weight range	Average (desirable)
25 to less than 30	Overweight	Increased
30 to less than 35	Obese class 1	Moderate
35 to less than 40	Obese class 2	Severe
40 or more	Obese class 3	Very severe

Source: Australian Institute of Health and Welfare (2004)

From Table 1, BMI beyond 30 has a lot of associated risks that can lead to health, social and psychological problems. BMI above 40 is dangerous and requires closer medical attention (Newbold, 2004). Overall, overweight and obesity entail health risks (Diertz, 1998) with potential effects to the social and economic wellbeing of an individual and the community at large. Poor health conditions resulting from overweight and obesity among children may act as a barrier to the development of a healthy mind, and thus pave the way to poor learning behaviours and outcomes (Rowland, 1990).

Some studies show that obese children are likely to experience social rejection and bullying from peers as well as teachers (Swan, 2002; Janssen, Craig, Boyce, & Pickett 2006; Trost 2007). Bullying and teasing of obese children undermine their academic potential and future social wellbeing (Jansen *et al.,* 2006). Understanding causes of overweight and obesity can help in identifying preventive measures, thus reducing the number of children likely to experience bullying at school.

In 2001, the Tanzanian government abolished competitive sports and physical education in schools (Bulamile, 2002). From this time new schools were being registered without meeting the criteria of having play grounds and reserved areas for sports and physical activities, where children can play. Although the situation was corrected in early 2008, many urban schools in Tanzania have neither a garden nor space for sports activities. Urban school children thus, have limited opportunity to participate in farming, sports or other physical activities, and so are becoming more vulnerable to overweight and obesity than their rural counterparts.

Participation in physical activities such as sports has a significant impact on the quality of children's lives. Mood, Musker & Rink (1995) argue that in order to provide and maintain optimum health, it is necessary for people of all ages to participate in physical exercise such as walking, jogging, swimming or cycling. Such activities are considered important to enhancing physical fitness and physical health as well as the development of cognitive ability. The ancient Greeks believed that a sound mind exists in a healthy body as Plato said, *"mens sana en corpore sano"* (cited in Rowland, 1990). According to Mabagala (2002), sports and physical activities have a potential role in the development of good physical health and fitness. It is also important in developing mental health and thus improving academic performance among school children (Mabagala, 2002).

The present study discusses the effects of overweight and obesity on learning behaviours and outcomes among primary school children in Tanzania. The study tested the following hypotheses:

i. There is no significant difference in prevalence of overweight and obesity between urban and rural primary school children.

ii. Overweight and obesity have no significant 'impact on the health and social wellbeing of primary school children

iii. Overweight and obesity have no significant impact on children's learning behaviours or outcomes.

This study, investigated obesity related health problems which had impacts on children learning behaviours and learning outcomes. Also it investigated social interaction between children who are overweight and obese, and those who are not. In addition, it proposed some control measure that can be taken by pareants and policy makers to minimize the impact of overweight and obesity in the country.

Effects of obesity on learning behaviours and outcomes

Overweight and obesity are reported to affect children's psychosocial outcomes, leading to low self-esteem and depression which together affect other aspects of children's lives, such as academic performance, with potentially even more serious long-term social outcomes (Swan, 2002). Datar, Sturm & Magnabosco (2004), reported that lower educational achievements among adults are associated with obesity while obese adolescents consider themselves worse students than 'normal-weight' students.

Social and psychological effects of obesity, which result from teasing and bullying, have also been undermining these children's academic performance (Datar *et al.*, 2004). Bullying is reported to be the highly prevalent (30%) form of aggression that involves repeated use of power and aggression. Social and psychological ramifications induced by bullying-victimization processes are reported to hinder the social development of overweight and obese children, since they are particularly reliant on peers for social support, identity, and self-esteem (Morrison, 2002). Janssen *et al* (2006) and Swan (2002) revealed that teachers also have negative attitudes toward obese children. Swan observes that teachers appear to pay less attention to overweight and obese children in the classroom than those who are not. According to Swan, both pre-service and in-service teachers perceive obese children more negatively than average-weight children. Rejection from teachers and peers causes the majority of overweight and obese children to drop out of school have higher levels of stress, anxiety, depression and illness which in turn affect children's academic performance records (Morrison, 2002).

Methodology

This study adopted a causal-comparative design to investigate the possible cause-and-effect relationship of overweight and obesity by observing existing consequences and searching back through data for plausible causal factors. Causal-comparative design was chosen as an ideal research design to investigate prevalence, and implications of overweight and obesity for children's health, social, learning behaviours and learning outcomes because it provided possibilities for assessing the cause of existing differences in learning behaviours and outcomes between obese and non-obese children. The sample for the study consisted of 4 primary schools, 4 teachers (one from each school) and 25 pupils not older than 14 years (from each school) in each district. A total of 8 schools, 8 teachers and 200 pupils participated in the study. Table 2 presents a summary of the participants' background characteristics

In order to determine the prevalence of overweight and obesity, data were collected by measuring children's weights and heights to determine BMI and measurement of skin folds to determine body fat percentage. Data on BMI and body fat percentages were important information for ascertaining the researcher that the population dealt with, was real overweight and obese. Opinions and experiences of teachers and students on the impacts of overweight obesity in children learning behaviours and outcomes were through questionnaires and interviews. Each research theme was studied by using more than one method (triangulation) so as to be certain with results. Table 2.1 shows different instruments used for data collection in each research themes.

Table 2: Data collection methods for each research theme

Research theme	Data collection method				
	Pupils' focus group discussion	Pupils questionnaire	Teachers' interviews	BMI measurement	Measurement of skinfolds
Prevalence				√	√
Causes		√	√		
Health and social	√	√	√		
Learning outcome	√	√	√		

Source: Adapted from Mafumiko (2006)

Validation of the research instruments was done by carrying out a pilot study in two schools in Dar es Salaam-one urban, one rural.

Findings and Discussion

Findings of this study are divided into three categories: social and health factors affecting children's learning; learning behaviours of overweight and obese children; and effects of overweight and obesity on academic performance.

Social and health factors affecting children's learning

Investigation on the social and health implications of overweight and obesity among primary school children were found to be insignificant for the following (see Table 3):

Social and health implications	Chi square, degree of freedom and significance level
Recurrent fevers	$\chi^2 = 1.59$, d.f $= 4$ and sig. $= 0.81$
Sleeping in the classroom	$\chi^2 = 2.68$, d.f $= 4$ and sig. $= 0.61$
Truancy	$\chi^2 = 5.31$, d.f $= 4$ and sig. $= 0.25$
Participation in sports	$\chi^2 = 1.75$, d.f $= 4$ and sig. $= 0.78$
Experiencing no problems	$\chi^2 = 3.53$, d.f $= 4$ and sig. $= 0.47$
Teasing and bullying.	$\chi^2 = 25.24$, d.f $= 4$ and sig. $= 0.00$

On average it was found that 85.2 percent of all overweight and obese children were experiencing teasing and bullying from their peers, 81.9 percent were unable to participate in sports and other physical activities, 25.9% were sleeping in the classroom, 19.4% were experiencing recurrent fever and body weaknesses, 9.7% were truant and only 6% were not experiencing any problem as shown in the Table 3.

Table 3: Problems experienced by Overweight and Obese Children

Social problem	Weight status	Frequency	Percentages	Sign.
Recurrent fever	Overweight	6	33.33	
	Obesity level I	2	25.00	0.81
	Obesity level II	0	0.00	
Sleep in class	Overweight	5	27.78	
	Obesity level I	4	50.00	0.61
	Obesity level II	0	0.00	
Truancy	Overweight	3	16.67	
	Obesity level I	1	12.50	0.25
	Obesity level II	0	0.00	
Can't partcipate in sports	Overweight	15	83.33	
	Obesity level I	5	62.50	0.78
	Obesity level II	1	100.00	
Teasing and bullying	Overweight	10	55.60	
	Obesity level I	8	100.00	0.01
	Obesity level II	1	100.00	
Noproblems	Overweight	1	5.56	
	Obesity level I	1	12.50	0.47
	Obesity level II	0	0.00	

Note: Results are presented on multiple responses bases.

Source: Kafyulilo (2008)

Results in Table 3, show that there were negligible amount of overweight and obese children who were not experiencing any problem. Majority of the children in the sample study were experiencing teasing and bullying as well as missing an opportunity to participate in sports and other physical activities (see also Morrison, 2002). It was also revealed that these children were experiencing heart problems and hypertension. Other children were experiencing excessive sweating and some were facing problems in breathing, as it was reported by a teacher in one of the urban schools that, "…I realize that these children's sweating levels is abnormal and sometimes they face difficulties even in breathing…"

The findings above are in line with those of Johnson (2002) who argues that excessive weight puts a great workload on the heart and circulatory systems causing a more profuse sweating and difficultness in breathing. Fat under skin prevents heat from escaping through the skin by sweating (Pangrazi, 1995). Grisogono (1991) argued that obese children are handicapped by their excessive weight, thus they require high oxygen uptake to do a given task.

Respiratory and breathing disorders frequently occur to overweight and obese children, due to problems of blood circulations caused by fat deposits around blood vessels (Pangrazi, 1995). WHO (2005) asserts that blood pressure increases with BMI. For every 10 kilogramme increase in weight, blood pressure rises by 2-3 mmHg. Conversely, weight loss induces a fall in blood pressure and typically, for each 1% reduction in body weight, blood pressure falls by 1-2 mmHg (WHO, 2005). Breathing difficultness may be resulting from high blood pressure, which induces high pressure in lungs, making it difficult for them to take air in and out smoothly.

Overweight and obese children were also found to be victims of discrimination and segregation from peers in various academic and social cultural activities. Likewise these children who are overweight and obese were reported to be the last to be chosen for any group work conducted in classroom or in other physical activities including sports. These findings support the argument of Gavin (2005) and Swan (2002) who argued that overweight and obese children have to bear the burden of discrimination from peers.

Findings from this study revealed also cases of grief between obese and non-obese children that existed in some schools as a result of teasing and bullying tendencies. In some schools, overweight and obese children were to comply with the teasing situation and adapt the names they were called, despite being awful. Names like "Bonge Nyanya (*big but weak like a tomato*)" "Mabofya (*sponge or soft thing*)", "Vitambi (*big stomach*)", "futufutu (*part of body extruding*)", "kipipa (*a canister/container*)", and "chura (*toad*)" were common to overweight and obese children. Worse enough these names were used by both teachers and students as it was observed also by Swan (2002). An example of practices associated with obesity and weight and how it affects children behaviours was testified by one obese child from one of the schools in Dar es Salaam, who said, *"...They just tease me; they call me "bonge (big)", and tell me that I should not be eating so much. May be they want me to stop eating blue band..."*

Some children were not used to those names and thus were getting angry and some of them abandoned school leading to children truancy (see also Morrison, 2002). More than 9% of overweight and obese children were not attending school because of the fear of being teased, bullied and the loneliness they experienced as a result of rejection from peers. Janssen *et al* (2006) reported that teasing and bullying were as high as 30% in school. These findings are also in-line with Swan, (2002) who observed that, when children were repeatedly bullied or teased, they started hating school.

Other weight related problems such as failure to arrive at school on time and failure to follow properly the teacher in classroom were further contributing to children truancies. Repeated punishments due to poor performance in various fields were also causing some overweight and obese children to put off school. However, not all overweight and obese children hated school; there were some who managed to cope with the situation thus maintaining their schooling programme.

Bullying and teasing by peers as well as teachers' negative attitudes towards overweight and obese children were pressing social and psychological problems which in turn affected their dynamism at school (see also Puhl, 2008). This study further revealed that obese children were quite unhappy with bullying and teasing tendencies. Yet more than 85% of overweight and obese children reported to have been bullied and teased. These findings were also similar to those of Swan (2002).

Apart from school drop-outs which were caused by overweight and obesity, over 80% of overweight and obese children were found to be not participating in sports activities. This was hindering them from social interactions with peers as well as limiting opportunities to express interest and talents they had in sports including other physical education programs. For example, about 75% of teachers and 68% of children contended that, obese children appeared to be afraid of carrying out simple activities in and outside the classroom for fear of being bullied or teased.

Learning behaviours of overweight and obese children

Due to health and social problems that overweight and obese children were experiencing in the course of learning, many of them were behaving different from others. Overall the following were mentioned as common health and social problems that overweight and obese children were experiencing and thus considered as their learning behaviours:

- Being inactive (laziness, shying away from actively participating in the lesson);
- Recurrent fevers which make them passive in the classroom;
- Sleeping in the class while the lesson is on;
- Breathing difficulties which makes them inactive;
- Too much sweating, and inability to interact with others in sports activities; Being teased and bullied which make them shy away to participate in some learning activities; and
- Others included being uneasy, failure to attend school at right time and sometimes truancy, appearing tired most of the time and self inferiority.

One of the urban school teachers for example, responded as follows; "…they are very lazy in performing various physical activities…"

When overweight and obese children were interviewed, they said they were not free to participate in sports and other physical activities. They faced problems in walking quickly and hence were reporting to school late. 30% of overweight children indicated to experience recurrent fevers such as headaches, colds and recurrent body weaknesses. These health conditions were making learning difficult for them. However, cases of heart diseases and high blood pressure were found to rarely exist among primary school children except four cases which were reported by some teachers to have existed in some schools.

Impact of overweight and obesity on academic performance

Results of the study showed a significant (χ^2 = 64.26, d.f = 16 and sig. = 0.000) impact of overweight and obesity on children's learning behaviours and outcomes. Majority were having poor or average academic performance. Interviews with teachers and children showed that overweight and obese children were more academic underperformers than normal weight and underweight children. One of the teachers from urban school indicated that, overweight children were slow in responding to questions in classrooms and were lazy in doing homework. Another teacher from rural schools said since he started teaching, he has never ever seen an obese child performing better in academic. Datar & Sturm (2006) and Texas department of Health (2004) report that overweight and obesity is associated with poor learning outcomes for school age children. This was evidenced by a teacher who said majority of overweight and obese children were poor or average in academic performance. His response is illustrated in the following in the following response:

"...they range from average to low performers. *I have never ever seen an overweight child getting the highest grades in academic.* They are not active, cannot stand up and attempt some questions in front of the class like others ..."

This argument was supported by a teacher from another school (school 4) who insisted that the performance of overweight and obese children in academic was either average or below average. She added that there were some overweight and obese children who were doing things quite contrary to their age level.

"...their performance is average, and there are some who are doing things contrary to their ages, they are too childish, different from the way peers of the same age are behaving..., ...most of the time they appear tired and inactive..."

About 87% of the interviewed teachers felt that, laziness, inactiveness and weakness that are experienced by overweight and obese children, were factors for their poor performance in academics. Examples of teachers' responses are:

"…these children are very lazy, not sharp … in the classroom they are inactive. They do not involve themselves in practical work. They do not like to participate in solving questions… Sometimes it is tiring when teaching obese children because they take a long time to understand…"

Another teachers said, "…overweight children take a long time to understand because they might be sleeping in the class or are not in good mood to respond to questions. They get tired to listen to the teacher …"

Further information on the relationship between weight status and children's learning behaviours and outcomes (academic performances) in grades is presented in Figure 1

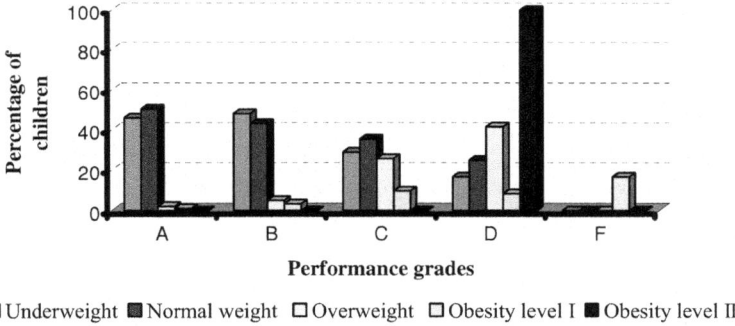

Figure 1: Children's Weight Status and their Academic Performance

Source: Kafyulilo (2008)

Figure 1, shows that, very fewer overweight and obese children were scoring "A" and "B" grade, whereas underweight and normal weight children were able to score A and B. Many overweight and obese children fell on the "C" grade; others fell on "D" and "F" grades.

It is not only in academic activities where overweight and obese children were underperforming, results showed that overweight and obese children were also achieving low in almost every activity they engaged in. Overweight and obese children were inactive in sport, social life and in academics. Over 67% of all overweight and obese children were having the least performance grades such as "D" and "F" (poor and failures respectively). Only few (about 12%) children in the study schools were getting the higher performance grades such as A, B and C.

Many studies (Datar *et al.*, 2004; Datar & Sturm, 2006; Swan, 2002; Janssen *et al.,* 2006) mentioned overweight and obesity as a hindrance to the children academic achievements. None of these studies articulated the way overweight and obesity affect the prosperity of the overweight and obesity in children learning behaviours and outcomes. This study revealed a number of reasons for overweight and obese children to have lower academic achievements than others. One was the lack of attention in the classroom due to poor body fitness thus laziness. The other was the tendency of overweight and obese children feeling tired almost every time and sleeping in the classroom. It was also revealed that poor health make up was making overweight and obese children uncomfortable with the studies when in the classroom. The consortium of those problems was subjecting the overweight and obese children into poor learning behaviours and finally affecting their learning outcomes.

Findings from the study revealed that overweight and obese children rarely participated in discussion with peers and were slow in responding to questions. They were also lazy and inactive when in the classroom. They arrived at school late getting to the classroom while others have already started studies. Some were experiencing excessive sweating especially in Dar es Salaam, thus failing to concentrate in the lesson when in the classroom.

Over 90% of teachers indicated that overweight and obese children were within the average and below average passes in academic subjects, results which comply with those of Datar *et al.* (2004) and Jansen *et al.,* (2006) who argued that overweight and obese children achieves less in education. Less than 10% of teachers said these children were performing well even better than normal weight children. The way these few teachers were arguing, it was reflecting that, they were very proud to have overweight and obese children in their school. This further implies that some teachers and guardians perceive overweight and obesity as a good health condition thus promoting it. But overweight and obese children themselves mention the situation as a hindrance to their better performance in academic.

About 34% of overweight and obese children agreed to be performing less in academics because of inability to seat for long time reading or doing rehearsal works. For example, it was revealed by this study that, overweight and obese children liked sleeping and watching television soon as they arrived at home from school, as illustrated in the following response;

"…I become weak in the class… even if I don't sleep in the class, but I sleep a lot at home… when I wake up, I don't feel well, I feel like going on sleeping…"

Along with the response above, overweight and obese children were the slowest in learning and inactive in responding to questions. This was witnessed by the researcher during the interview with overweight and obese children that it was taking long for a question to be answered when an obese child was appointed to answer it.

In view of these findings the null hypothesis which stated that, "overweight and obesity have no significance implications on children learning behaviours and outcomes" was rejected.

Conclusions and Recommendations

The aim of this study was to contribute to existing literature on physical education and health on the effects of overweight and obesity in school children's learning behaviours and academic performance. The findings presented and discussed in this study show that overweight and obesity have significant impact not only on health but also on social and academic affairs, thus a concern for educators and stakeholders in other sectors such as health and sport. In fact, weight control is a rational task, which is not easy to everyone. Therefore, commitment, motivation and sufficient information are keys to successful weight control through physical activities and diet manipulations. Development and introduction of education programs that will address issues related to overweight and obesity is paramount for building a generation with a health body and health mind. This may include educating parents and other stakeholders in education, sports and health through Media, such as Radios, News papers, Television and internet programmes.

Stakeholders in education, sports and health should put a mechanism that will guide all children at schools to participate in physical activities. Such activities may include sports and other domesticated activities that in turn will act as an outlet for excessive body fat deposits. This will help in improving body health conditions and academic performance. The common goal of children's wellness and fitness should help physical education become an integral part of total school curricula. Schools should be equipped with relevant facilities and equipment necessary for improving body movement skills as well as fitness among school children. Parents, teachers, guardians and other stakeholders in education, sports and health should make efforts to ensure that physical education programs are not only part of the curricula but also a compulsory component of education programmes at all levels.

Also policies on sports and physical education should be restated so as to incorporate criteria for all children of all ages in sports and health related activities. The policy statement should provide an open room for parents, guardians and stakeholders in education to debate on how to develop children's interests towards physical activities, sports and development of good sportsmanship.

Education policies should also put sports and leisure activities as a compulsory component of education, since they have an important attribute in the development of the whole human body. Leisure activities and exercises are very important component in development of the child's physical, mental and intellectual characteristics (Rowland, 1990). Therefore, policies on education should view physical education and sports as a foundation stone towards children with good body health and minds, together with well developed intellectual and physical capabilities.

References

Australian Institute of Health and Welfare. (2004). *What are the Preventable Risk Factors for Cardiovascular Disease?* www.aihw.gov.au/riskfactors Retrieved on Friday, 28th December, 2007

Bulamile, N.M. (2002). *Physical Education for People with Hearing Impairments: A Case Study of a School for the Deaf in Tanzania.* Unpublished, M.A (Education) Dissertation, Dar es Salaam, University of Dar es Salaam

Datar A and Sturm R. (2006). Childhood overweight and elementary school outcomes. *International Journal of Obesity,* 30, 1449–1460

Datar, A., Sturm, R., & Magnabosco, F. (2004). "Childhood Overweight and Academic Performance: National Study of Kindergartners and First-Graders", *Obesity Research,* Vol 1, No. 12. 113-138

Diertz, L. (1998). *Health-related Physical Fitness in Childhood: Status and Recommendations.* Annu: Rev Public Health

Ekblom, O. (2005). *Physical Fitness and Overweight in Swedish Youths.* Stockholm: Reproprint AB

Gavin, M. (2005). *Overweight and Obesity,* www.childhealth.org/parents/general Retrieved on Friday, 26th January, 2007

Grisogono, V. (1991). *Children and Sport.* London: John Murray publishers limited

Johnson, E. (2002). *Prevalence and Trends of Overweight and Obesity among US Children and Adolescents.* www.cdc.gov/nchs/products/overweight Retrieved on Friday, 20th January, 2007

Janssen, I., Craig, W., Boyce, W., & Pickett, W. (2006). "Association between Overweight and Obesity with Bullying Behaviours in School-Aged Children", *Official Journal of the American Academy of Paediatrics, Vol 5, No.113, 233-246*

Kafyulilo, A. C. (2008). Prevalence and Implications of Overweight and Obesity in Children's Health and Learning Behaviour: The Case of Kinondoni and Njombe Districts. Master Dissertation, Dar es Salaam, University of Dar es salaam

Mabagala, S. (2002). *Psychological Determinants of Young People's Participation in Sports and Physical Activities.* Unpublished M.A (Education) Dissertation, Dar es Salaam, University of Dar es Salaam

Mafumiko, F. (2006). *Micro-scale Experimentation as a Catalyst for Improving the Chemistry Curriculum in Tanzania.* Enschede: PrintPartners Ipskamp

Mood, D., Musker, F., & Rink, J. (1995). *Sports and Recreational Activities.* Boston: WCB/McGraw-Hill

Morrison, B. (2004). *Bullying and Victimization in Schools: A Restorative Justice Approach.* Cannibera, A ustralian Institute of Criminology.

Newbold, R. (2004). *Overview of Clinical Perspectives and Mechanisms of Obesity* in *Developmental Origins and Environmental Influences.* Duke: Duke University

Pangrazi, R. P. (1995). *Dynamic Physical Education for Elementary School Children.* Allyn: Bacon publishers

Puhl, R. (2008). Obese youth: Vulnerable Targets of Stigma and Teasing. Rudd Center for Food Policy and Obesity. Yale University.
http://www.wlslifestyles.com/cached/_downloads/2867/Obese%20Youth%20Vulnerable%20Targets%20of%20Stigma%20and%20Teasing%20MAIN.pdf
Retrieved on 27th December 2009

Rowland T.W (1990). *Exercise and Children's Health.* Illinois, Human Kinetics Books

Swan, Y.G. (2002). *Examining Academic and Social Bias of Educators towards Overweight Students in the Classroom.* Unpublished M.Sc (Health Science) dissertation, Menomonie, University of Wisconsin-Stout

Sharkey, B. J. (1997). *Fitness and Health.* New York: Human kinetics publishers

Texas Department of Health. (2004). *Psychological Impact of Obesity on School-aged Children.*
http://www.dshs.state.tx.us/obesity/pdf/psychological%20impact%20of%20obesity.pdf Retrieved on 15th January 2010.

World Health Organization. (2005). *Facing the Facts about BMI, Overweight and Obesity Statistics in Tanzania.* www.who.int/en Retrieved Tuesday, 23rd December, 2006

Lightning Source UK Ltd.
Milton Keynes UK
UKOW04f0608190917

309457UK00001B/177/P

9 783656 205838